DIARY

OF A
MINECRAFT
ZOMBIE

Book 1

Zack Zombie

Monday

"**U**uuuurrrgghhhh!!!"

"Honey, it's time to get up!"

"Uuuurrrgghhhaacckkhuhh?"

"Honey, it's night time already, you need to get up!"

"Aww Mom, do I have to?"

"Yes, you do. Those villagers aren't going to scare themselves."

"Uuuurrgghhhhh!!!"

"Don't *Uuuuurrrgghhh* Me. You get up, and get ready this instant!"

"OK Mom."

Zombie parents can be a real pain sometimes.

It's always, "Do this," and "Scare that."

Some days I wish I were human so I wouldn't have to get up at night and go scaring.

I'm sure human parents aren't like this.

And I'm sure human parents aren't always telling their kids what to do.

Human parents are probably really nice and let their kids stay up all day and do whatever they want.

But not Zombie parents.

"Don't go out during the day because you'll burn yourself! Blah, blah, blah," they say.

One day, I'm just going to stay out all day, just to see what will happen.

My friend Creepy stays out during the day and nothing happens to him.

As a matter of fact, so does Slimey next door.

Urrggghhhh! They have all the fun. Why can't my parents be like that?

Well, at least I'm not alone. My best friend Skelee can't go out during the day, either. His parents are really strict.

Skelee's parents won't even let him have a dog.

He said his uncle got a dog once, but it buried his grandmother in the back yard.

And they never found her.

Bummer...

Tuesday

Well, it's a scare day today, so I have to go out and scare some villagers again.

Most of the time it's boring, but sometimes it can be fun.

One time, I crept up behind a villager and put my arms out like this, and said, "Uurrrgghhh!!!"

It really scared him.

Actually, he was so scared he ran away and dropped his sword.

I took it as a souvenir. I have it hanging up on my wall.

Another time, I was in a friendly mood, and I said, "Hi!" to a villager.

He fainted.

I think it was my breath.

Mom always tells me not to brush my teeth. But today I forgot and did anyway.

Wednesday

There's a Zombie at school that really gets on my nerves.

No really, he steps on the nerves on my feet every time he walks by.

His name is Jeff.

I wouldn't be so mad if he wasn't bragging all of the time.

"I scared five villagers yesterday," he said really loud in my face.

"Who cares? Anybody can do that."

"And I did it during the daytime!" he said.

"What! During the daytime?!!!"

"Yep, during the daytime!"

Either he was lying or Jeff is not such a lame brain after all.

He said that his uncle took him out on a rainy day, and they scared a bunch of villagers that were huddled under a tree.

I still don't believe him.

But it would explain why he smells funny.

Zombies aren't supposed to get wet.

At Scare School today, the teacher taught us about the best time to scare villagers.

He said if we're really lucky we could catch a villager trying to mine at night.

They're great, because they always drop cool stuff you can take home.

My buddy Creepy said his uncle scared a miner one night. He almost went home with a fat diamond.

But his uncle got so excited, he blew up.

Thursday

After Scare School, me, Creepy, Skelee and Slimey like to go out to have some fun.

Sometimes we go to the village to cause some trouble.

Our favorite game is to bang on some doors and run away.

I almost got caught once.

But I just said, "Uuurrrrgghhh" to talk my way out of it.

Worked like a charm.

Creepy told me that he came face to face with a villager once.

He got so nervous he started shaking.

He tried to introduce himself, but the guy just ran away.

I don't think people really get Creepy.

My favorite game is Hide and Seek.

Our friend Slimey told us he played hide and seek with his uncle once.

One time his uncle hid in the water.

They never heard from him again.

Friday

I got home from school and my little brother started bothering me again.

He's such a little ankle biter!

No, really.

He likes to bite my ankles and run away...
Really fast!

Sometimes he hops on his chicken, and then I can never catch him.

Mom says I used to do the same thing when I was his age.

I guess they don't feed us enough when we're kids.

My Mom said I had to get ready for dinner.

I asked her, "What's for dinner tonight?"

"Rotten meatloaf."

"Can't we go out to eat?" I asked her.

"There are no villagers out tonight. So no, we can't!"

Bummer. I was really hungry…

I know what you're thinking.

But we don't eat villagers.

But when we scare them, they sometimes drop really yummy food.

One time, I scared a villager and she dropped a cake!

That was the best day ever.

Saturday

Today, Mom says we're going to my cousin's house.

He lives in the Nether.

It wouldn't be so bad if it wasn't so hot there all the time.

My cousin's name is Piggy.

Funny name, right?

Piggy doesn't think so...

When I asked Piggy where he was from, he
told me something about his dad being struck
by lightning or something like that.

Piggy is always making stuff up.

Piggy's house is right in the middle of the
Nether.

The Nether is a nice place to visit, but I wouldn't want to live there.

The first time I visited, I brought my sleeping bag.

I rolled it out to get ready for bed and… Boom!

I'm never going to do that again.

Also, it's really noisy there.

Too much snorting and wailing.

Mom tells me it's just the Ghasts that do a fly by once in a while.

They're really noisy for flying octopuses.

Piggy introduced me to his friend Blaze.

16

I tried to give him a high five, but he didn't have any hands...

Talk about awkward!

Piggy and I play all kinds of games.

But the only game we can't play is tag.

As soon as I tag Piggy, all of his relatives get mad and start chasing me for some reason.

Sunday

Contrary to what most people think, humans can be friendly.

I actually have a human friend.

His name is Steve.

We have a lot in common.

Steve is kind of weird looking. He has a square head.

Steve also never changes his clothes.

And I thought only Zombies did that!

Steve walks funny too.

I tried walking like him once.

And a villager started talking to me.

I didn't know what to do.

So I ran away.

But even though he's weird, Steve is still my friend.

My mom says I shouldn't make friends with humans.

She says they smell funny.

Plus, she says, "If the humans become our friends, who are we going to scare?"

She didn't like my idea about scaring little brothers.

My mom doesn't like me asking her too many questions, either.

One day I asked her, "Mommy, where do Zombies come from?"

She seemed a bit tongue tied.

But then I remembered she doesn't have a tongue!

When she finally said something, she said, "Zombies are mobs created by computer programmers at Mojang to make the game of Minecraft a more challenging and enjoyable experience."

Whenever my Mom uses big words, I know she's hiding something.

My friend Creepy said that Zombies come from being bitten by other infected Zombies, a plague that originated from some secret military experiment.

I think Creepy watches too much television.

I liked Skelee's answer the best.

He says Zombies aren't made, they're born.

He said they hatch from eggs.

Kinda' makes sense. I've seen a lot of eggs around here.

Monday

Sometimes, after school, me and the guys go out to mess with the spiders.

They don't do much. They just crawl around.

But we like to tip them over.

I saw some humans do that to a cow once.

It looked like fun.

But, you need to be careful with cave spiders.

They get really mad if you tip them over.

They think they're better than regular spiders.

I found out the hard way that you shouldn't tip over a silverfish.

They travel in gangs.

It wasn't much fun getting beat up by silverfish.

23

Tuesday

I like the Endermen.

They're really nice.

They're also really tall for teenagers.

24

But I still can't understand what they do all night.

I guess moving blocks around is fun.

I just don't get it.

It's probably a secret club, and only the coolest kids can be a part of it.

I tried talking to one to find out the inside scoop.

It didn't work.

He just stared at me.

I wish I could travel like Endermen.

They don't have to walk.

They just teleport wherever they want to go.

If I could do that, I would teleport to grandma's house every day.

She always has the best snacks.

My favorite is when she makes lady fingers….

…the sandwiches I mean.

Wednesday

We have a witch that lives on our street.

I think she's funny looking.

She has a big nose with a mole on it.

She walks around mad all of the time.

I would be mad too if I had a big nose with a mole on it.

One day Skelee asked the witch what it's like to have a big nose with a mole on it.

She just walked away…mad.

The kids in the neighborhood sometimes tease her and say she's ugly.

Mom says the witch probably looked better when she was younger.

So, me and the guys decided to look up her year book in the school library...

28

Nope, she's always been ugly.

I wonder what it's like to have a nose.

Dad says I had an uncle who had a nose.

He got a cold once.

And that's the last time they ever saw his nose again.

Dad also said that I had another uncle who had ears.

He couldn't find them after he started wearing a helmet.

Thursday

I used to feel embarrassed when my body parts occasionally fell off.

Now, it's the best excuse ever for staying home from school!

It doesn't happen often.

But when it does, I milk it for all it's worth.

I just have to pick the right body parts.

One time I said, "Mom, I just lost an eyeball!"

"Congratulations Honey!" she said.

But now, I stick to the legs.

Can't go to school without legs.

Mom says that when a Zombie loses a tooth, they can put it under their pillow and the tooth fairy will come and give you a quarter.

I thought I struck it rich, until I realized that the most I can ever make is seventy-five cents.

Friday

Mom and Dad said that if I get a good grade on my Scare test, I can get a pet.

That sounded awesome until I realized I could only get a pet squid.

I would rather have a cat or a dog, like Steve.

But Mom says we can't because we shed all over the furniture.

"Dogs have a habit of burying our body parts in the back yard," she says.

"Cats are worse. They have a habit of turning everything into a scratching post."

Squids are OK, I guess. But all they do is swim around.

Creepy's parents gave him a pig.

Now that's a cool pet.

He didn't have it for long though.

One day it got struck by lightning.

My cousin Piggy thought he saw it roaming around his neighborhood in the Nether.

Speaking of lightning, one of Creepy's uncles got struck by lightning once.

They took him to the hospital.

He didn't stay long, though.

The hospital exploded.

I think the witch on our street was struck by lightning once, too.

It probably hit her on the nose.

I guess if I got struck by lightning, I'd be mad too.

Saturday

My uncle Wither is coming to visit today.

I wouldn't mind, but he usually makes such a mess!

I tried sneaking up on him once.

I couldn't do it.

He seems to always know when I'm coming.

I'm not going to be able to stay long, though.

I want to go see Skelee's older brother's new band.

They call themselves The Walking Dead.

36

Cool.

Mom doesn't like them.

She says they're a bad influence.

She says if I keep listening to music like that I'll start acting more human.

Uncle Wither told me he was in a band once.

I thought it was a rock band.

Turned out it was Obsidian.

Not cool.

Sunday

I'd thought I would go visit Steve today.

Steve sometimes likes to mine at night.

I think I'm going to creep up to him and scare him today.

But he usually hears me coming.

Steve says he wants to be a Zombie like me.

He says Zombies have the easy life.

Boy, if he only knew...

I tried to introduce Steve to my friends.

But Creepy got really nervous around him.

So we had to put Creepy on a time out.

Steve and Skelee got along really well.

They even played cowboys and Indians.

Steve is usually the cowboy.

I know because when they're finished, Steve's usually covered in arrows.

Today Steve asked me how you can tell a girl Zombie from a boy Zombie.

I said, "That's easy. All you have to do is look at our clothes."

Steve just looked at me, confused.

He asked me if Zombies had girlfriends.

"Yeah, they do."

Then he asked me if I had a Zombie girlfriend.

I said, "Of course I do! What do you think I am, a loser?"

The truth is, I don't have a girlfriend.

But Sally Cadaver, from biology class, has been in each of my classes since second grade, so "technically" I can call her my girlfriend.

"How do you kiss, since you don't have lips?" Steve asked.

I just looked at Steve, confused.

Monday

A few weeks ago a new kid transferred to my school.

His name is Jake.

He's a Wither Skeleton.

They say he got kicked out of his last school because he poisoned somebody.

I think I'm going to make friends with him so that if anyone messes with me, Jake could threaten to poison them too.

I just hope he doesn't poison me first.

But, it's always good to have someone like Jake on your side.

You see, being a Zombie in middle school can be a dangerous thing.

Sometimes you need protection.

Especially from bullies.

The biggest bully in school is a kid named Mike Magma.

He's a Magma Cube.

Everybody says he's a real hot-head.

What's weird is that Mike is Slimey's cousin, and he picks on Slimey too.

I wonder what kind of poison Jake would use on him.

Well, a kid can wish, can't he?

Tuesday

Today the class went to a new village to practice scaring.

I was a little nervous because Jeff said this village had an Iron Golem.

If you don't know what an Iron Golems is, just imagine a giant foot designed for the sole purpose of squashing a Zombie like a cockroach.

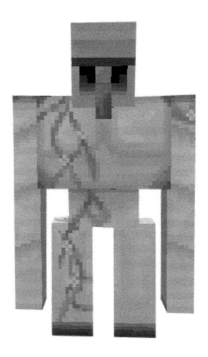

Jeff said no Zombie had ever seen one and lived to tell about it.

Our teacher Ms. Bones heard our conversation and told us that there were no Iron Golems at the village.

Still, I like my limbs, and I would like to keep them, thank you.

Creepy got nervous and started shaking again.

Ms. Bones decided to send him home with a note.

The village was actually quite peaceful.

There were no villagers out so I practiced scaring some sheep.

Didn't work very well.

They just stood there looking at me.

Wednesday

Today I got caught passing a note to Skelee in class.

It wouldn't be so bad if today wasn't the day that Skelee wanted to know who I liked.

And it wouldn't be so bad if we had one of those laid back, nice teachers.

But Ms. Bones is as stiff as they come.

She has a rule that if she catches anyone passing notes in her class, she's going to read it out loud to everybody.

And today, she read out loud that, "I LIKE SALLY CADAVER AND I WANT HER TO BE MY GIRLFRIEND."

My life is officially over…

The only thing that saved me was that Sally was out for the week because she was getting her tonsils put back in.

But now the whole school knows!

Including Jeff.

Knowing Jeff, he's going to try to beat me at getting Sally as a girlfriend.

Ever since we were kids, Jeff is always trying to show that he's better than me at something.

Jeff was the first to lose his baby teeth…and his regular teeth.

Jeff was the first to grow mold on his chest.

Jeff was also the first to get a villager to faint during scare practice.

It wouldn't be so bad, but Jeff is better looking than me too.

He's lost more hair than I have.

He's a nicer shade of green than I am.

And he's got more of his guts and entrails showing than I do.

He'll have Sally Cadaver as his girlfriend in no time.

I'm doomed.

Thursday

After what happened yesterday, I decided to fake being sick to stay home from school.

Usually a missing limb would do the trick, but I think my Mom and Dad were on to me.

So I decided to use my ace in the hole…

I was going to take a bath!

Zombies are not supposed to get wet.

And Zombies are definitely not supposed to take baths!

It takes a lot of years to get your rotting flesh just the right color and smell.

Taking a bath would make you look like you were, "The Living."

The perfect effect I wanted.

Mom and Dad didn't know that I knew about baths.

I learned it from Steve.

He says humans take baths all the time.

That would explain why Mom says that humans smell funny.

So right before evening, when the moon was about to rise, I woke up early, sneaked out of the house and ran to the lake.

"This is it," I thought.

As I was looking at the lake, and getting myself ready to jump in, Old Man Jenkins came out riding his Zombie horse.

"Whaddya think you're doing, young man?"

"I'm about to take a bath!" I said.

"What in tarnation would you do that for?"

So, I told him the whole story.

As weird as it was, I could tell he knew from first-hand experience what I was going through.

I guess all Zombies have to go through this stuff as kids.

Then old man Jenkins said, "Just wash your hand and tell your Mom and Dad you caught a rash at school. Always worked for me."

So I tried it...

Worked like a charm!

Now I just have to find another idea of how to stay home from school tomorrow.

Friday

Today I washed the other hand and told my Mom and Dad that the rash had spread.

They believed it.

Only problem is, they believed it too well.

My Mom and Dad rushed me to the hospital so that the doctor could check to see if I was turning human.

They even called a specialist to see if I was contagious.

Great, not only do the kids at school think I'm an outcast, the whole neighborhood will too, I thought.

The specialist was a witch doctor from the Swamp Biome.

I didn't know that men could be witches too.

But there he was, with a big nose with a mole on it.

After checking me out, he sent me home.

I think the witch doctor knew I was faking.

Probably because he had to do the same thing when he was a kid.

Skelee, Creepy and Slimey came over to see how I was doing.

Creepy was nervous of catching what I had, so he started shaking again.

The guys sent him home because the pressure was too much for him.

I asked the guys how it went at school.

54

"They sent everyone home because some kid at school caught the 'White Hand' disease."

"Do they know who it was?" I asked.

"Nope."

"What's wrong with you, anyway?" Skelee asked.

"Just a cold," I said, as I slowly covered my hands.

Saturday

After my miraculous one day recovery, Dad decided to take me on a camping trip.

He wanted to take me to the Swamp Biome.

He said the stale air would do me some good.

Dads like to take their kids on camping trips, thinking that it will do them good.

Slimey's dad took him to the Snowy Biome once.

I don't think he thought it through, though.

They were frozen solid for a few days until they were discovered by some tourists.

Skelee's Dad took him to the forest biome.

Afterwards, he said he wasn't expecting there to be so many wolves.

Creepy's Dad took him and the whole family on a field trip to the Desert Biome.

Nobody warned them about the Cactus.

Now, I'm not saying Dads don't mean well.

It's just that they don't have a great track record when it comes to preparing for these trips.

Moms on the other hand, prepare for everything.

My Mom even gave me some bug spray so that the Swamp bugs would lay eggs on me on my trip.

Dad didn't think of that.

Sunday

Today I went to go visit Steve.

He was busy punching a tree.

I was going to ask him what he was doing, but I'm used to seeing him do weird things like that.

"What's eating you?" Steve said.

59

"Maggots. How about you?"

"No, I mean what's bothering you?" he said.

So I told him the whole story about Sally Cadaver.

"Wow, Zombies and humans aren't very different," Steve said.

"We smell different."

"Yeah, that's true," Steve said. "But on the inside, we're exactly the same."

I just looked at Steve, confused.

Steve smiled and went back to punching his tree.

I went home and I decided that today, I wanted to test how strong I am.

I was going to show Jeff that I can do anything he can.

So, I decided to go out during the day.

Creepy's coming with me to take pictures, so I can prove I did it.

Hey, if Steve could punch a tree… I can do this!

Monday

Stayed home from school today to grow my skin back.

Ouch.

Tuesday

Back to school today.

I was bummed because I wanted to skip another day of school.

But rotten flesh grows back pretty fast.

I guess it's not so bad, because today we're going on a field trip.

But field trips can be a hit or miss sometimes.

Ms. Bones took us to an abandoned mine once.

It was cool, but Skelee got lost and we couldn't find him for days.

He said he got kidnapped by some blood thirsty humans that wanted to eat his brains.

But I think he just got stuck in a spider web and was too embarrassed to tell anyone.

Especially since Skelee doesn't have blood or a brain.

Ms. Bones said that we were taking a trip to the Ender World.

That's where the Endermen live.

This is great because I can finally settle a bet with Slimey over what an Enderman house looks like.

Slimey says it's probably a castle made of Obsidian and diamonds.

I think it's probably more like a junkyard since they are always picking up blocks of stuff.

Ms. Bones said we may even see the Enderdragon.

That would be so cool.

I heard about the Enderdragon.

It's supposed to be this massively awesome dragon that flies around in the Ender World.

My Dad said that he saw it fly by once.

But I think my Dad made that up just to look cool.

I think the older you get, the harder Dads work at trying to be cool.

Wednesday

The field trip yesterday was a total bomb.

Nobody told me that it was a field trip to the Ender World Natural Museum.

The Enderdragon was just an exhibit of some old dinosaur bones.

It's just like teachers to ruin a kid's dream.

And, the only Enderman I met was the security guard that was guarding the Ender Crystal exhibit.

But I have to admit, the Enderdragon exhibit was pretty awesome.

They only had a skeleton of the Enderdragon, but it was huge!

Skelee was drooling.

Thursday

After class today, I saw Sally Cadaver.

She was talking to big mouth Jeff.

I wanted to say hi, and see if I could take my relationship with her to the next level.

But Jeff started bragging again.

"I saw an Iron Golem with my uncle yesterday!" he said.

"Big deal," I said.

I knew I had to step up my game, or my feeble chances to make Sally my girlfriend would be utterly crushed.

"Yeah, well... I actually touched one!" I said.

Mouths opened. Books dropped. I heard creaking noises as heads turned towards me.

Oh man. I really stepped in it now.

I knew the next words out of Jeff's mouth were going to determine the fate of my existence for all eternity.

"I dare you to do it again!" Jeff said.

He said it! I was doomed.

"OK," I said, thinking that I might have enough time to get out of town.

But Sally looked at me like I was the Enderdragon himself. So you know I had to open my big mouth, and say, "When and where. Just name it!"

"Tomorrow night," Jeff said.

Great, I have one day left to live...

Friday

Today is the day.

Today is the day I face my death at the hands of an Iron Golem.

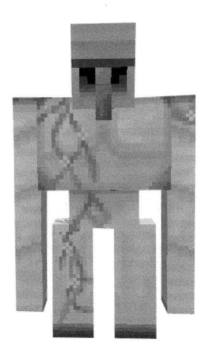

I went downstairs and gave my Mom and Dad a farewell hug.

They didn't know that today would be my last day to live, but I didn't have the heart to tell them.

My little brother was riding his chicken around too fast so I didn't get a chance to say goodbye to him either.

After school, Jeff had his uncle take us to where they saw the Iron Golem before.

And sure enough, there it was, standing guard in front of the village.

Everybody from school was there, too.

Great, I'm gonna die, and there's gonna be an audience.

My family's name will be cursed forever.

70

There was Sally, looking at me through her big eye sockets, so proud of the Zombie that I had become.

Well, at least she can enjoy it for the next few short minutes of my life, I thought.

"OK, it's time," Jeff said.

Gulp!

Well, here it goes…

I started walking toward the Iron Golem.

As I started walking, it looked at me and got into a Zombie squashing stance.

"Oh man, this is going to hurt," I said under my breath.

My Dad told me that when he was in the Zombie Army, he got hit by an Iron Golem once.

He said it took them weeks to find his left arm and leg.

All this for Sally Cadaver.

Man, girls are just trouble!

I was just about within arm's reach of the Iron Golem when I thought to myself, "This is dumb. Who am I kidding? I'm a loser."

I started to turn around in utter shame when all of a sudden Steve jumped out from behind the Iron Golem.

The crowd went silent.

Then Steve came over to me and put his arm around my shoulder, and walked me to the Iron Golem.

The Iron Golem lifted up his hand like he planned to crush the both of us with a single blow…

Then when his hand came down...It was full of flowers!

He gave them to me and Steve, and I took some.

The crowd was so surprised, I think some of them dropped their jaws literally.

I walked back to the crowd of mobs and handed the flowers to Sally.

Everybody started cheering.

I turned around and gave Steve a thumbs up.

And He gave me one back.

73

Saturday

Yesterday was the best day ever.

I survived being crushed by an Iron Golem.

I proved to Jeff that I am better at something than he is.

And Sally Cadaver is no longer "technically" my girlfriend. Now she "is" my girlfriend.

But I still wish someone would tell me how I'm supposed to kiss her with no lips.

Everybody is talking about what happened yesterday, too.

But the thing that people are really talking about is how I have a human friend named Steve.

Guess the secret's out.

Well, I hope more Zombies can find friends like Steve.

Then instead of going out scaring villagers at night...

We could all just get along.

Sunday

Today, Steve invited me to come visit his village.

I'm going to bring Skelee, Creepy and Slimey with me.

I think it's going to be a lot of fun.

Creepy was a little scared, though.

Had to calm him down.

I don't know why he's so scared.

I mean really… What could go wrong?

Find out What
Happens Next in...

Diary of a Minecraft Zombie Book 2
"Bullies and Buddies"

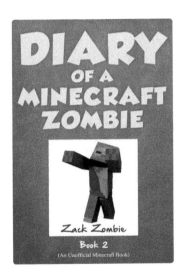

Get Your Copy and Join Zombie on
More Exciting Adventures!

If you really liked this book, please tell a friend. I'm sure they will be happy you told them about it.

Leave Us a Review Too

Please support us by leaving a review. The more reviews we get the more books we will write!

Check Out All of Our Books in the Diary of a Minecraft Zombie Series

The Diary of a Minecraft Zombie Book 1
"A Scare of a Dare"

In the first book of this hilarious Minecraft adventure series, take a peek in the diary of an actual 12 year old Minecraft Zombie and all the trouble he gets into in middle school.

Get Your Copy Today!

The Diary of a Minecraft Zombie Book 2
"Bullies and Buddies"

This time Zombie is up against some of the meanest and scariest mob bullies at school. Will he be able to stop the mob bullies from terrorizing him and his friends, and make it back in one piece?

Jump into the Adventure and Find Out!

The Diary of a Minecraft Zombie Book 3
"When Nature Calls"

What does a Zombie do for Spring break?
Find out in this next installment of the exciting
and hilarious adventures of a 12 year old
Minecraft Zombie!

Get Your Copy Today!

The Diary of a Minecraft Zombie Book 4
"Zombie Swap"

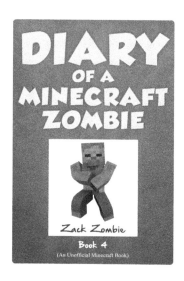

12 Year Old Zombie and Steve
have Switched Bodies!
Find out what happens as 12 year old
Zombie has to pretend to be human and
Steve pretends to be a zombie.

Jump into this Zany
Adventure Today!

The Diary of a Minecraft Zombie Book 5
"School Daze"

Summer Vacation is Almost Here and
12 Year Old Zombie Just Can't Wait!
Join Zombie on a Hilarious Adventure as
he tries to make it through the last few
weeks before Summer Break.

Jump into the
Adventure Today!

The Diary of a Minecraft Zombie Book 6
"Zombie Goes To Camp"

Join 12 year old Zombie, as he faces his biggest fears, and tries to survive the next 3 weeks at Creepaway Camp.
Will he make it back in one piece?

Jump into His Crazy Summer Adventure and Find Out!

86

The Diary of a Minecraft Zombie Book 7
"Zombie Family Reunion"

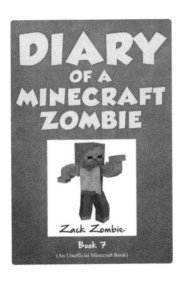

Join Zombie and his family on their crazy
adventure as they face multiple challenges
trying to get to their 100th Year
Zombie Family Reunion.
Will Zombie even make it?

Get Your Copy Today
and Find Out!

The Diary of a Minecraft Zombie Book 8
"Back to Scare School"

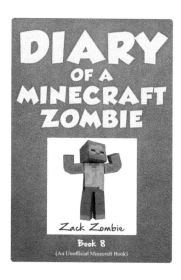

Zombie finally made it through 7th grade...
And he even made it through one really crazy
summer! But will Zombie be able to survive
through the first weeks of being an 8th grader
in Mob Scare School?

Find Out in His Latest Adventure Today!

The Diary of a Minecraft Zombie Book 9
"Zombie's Birthday Apocalypse"

It's Halloween and it's Zombie's Birthday!
But there's a Zombie Apocalypse happening that
may totally ruin his Birthday party. Will Zombie
and his friends be able to stop the Zombie
Apocalypse so that they can finally enjoy some
cake and cookies at Zombie's Birthday Bash?

Jump into the Adventure
and Find Out!

The Diary of a Minecraft Zombie Book 10
"One Bad Apple"

There's a new kid at Zombie's middle
school and everyone thinks he is so cool.
But the more Zombie hangs out with him, the
more trouble he gets into. Is this new Mob kid
as cool as everyone thinks he is, or is he really a
Minecraft Wolf in Sheep's clothing?

Jump Into this Zany Minecraft Adventure and Find Out!

90

CPSIA information can be obtained
at www.ICGtesting.com
Printed in the USA
LVHW111635231221
706905LV00002B/25

9 781943 330089